DEGAS

DEGAS

BY

GEORGES CHARENSOL

OLDBOURNE PRESS
LONDON

Great movements in the arts, whether in painting or literature, show an appearance of unity only to the eyes of posterity. It is easy to see that those comparatively close to our own day – the Nabis, Fauves, or Cubists – will last for a few years. Some paths cross, while chance or similarity relate some artists to one another, as Picasso and Braque to Collioure, or Derain and Vlaminck to Chatou. It may come about that a gallery or an exhibition brings together a number of works roughly related in spirit and tendency, as in 1905 when the Salon d'Automne took charge of the Fauves. But immediately afterwards Matisse, Vlaminck, Dufy, Derain, Friesz, Rouault, Camoin went their own way, and it is quite impossible to treat this chance collection of painters as a school of painting. Yet the passage of time inspires a systematic treatment of complex matters – which is the reason why Degas is today still classed with the Impressionists.

THE IMPRESSIONISTS

The first impulse which brought together these painters so different in temperament was the friendship between Bazille, Monet, Renoir and Sisley. They met at the Gleyre studios in 1863, the year of the scandal provoked by Edouard Manet's masterpiece, *The Picnic,* which was turned down by the hanging committee of the official Salon, to become the sensation of the Salon des Refusés. People went to see it at the Palais de l'Industrie, to laugh, express their indignation, or show their enthusiasm. It was there that the young painters working at Gleyre's or the Academy Suisse made the discovery that one of their elders had opened up a new path, working direct from nature with a bold use of colour, as did the disregarded painters of the Barbizon school, whom they were to follow both in their fierce independence and in the simplicity of their lives.

At Suisse's in 1861, Paul Cézanne made the acquaintance of Guillaumin and Francesco Oller. But his meeting with Pissarro was the chief benefit that he was to draw from his time at this academy. From 1866 onwards, all these painters used to go to the Café Guerbois, where Manet was the leading spirit and where the future Impressionists played a humbler role, lost among a crowd of artists and writers better known than themselves.

Among these painters there was one who had first exhibited in the Salon of 1865 with a *Medieval Battlefield* in a very traditional style. Doubtless Edgar Degas had been led to the Café Guerbois by Manet or possibly some critic who had noticed the painting he sent to a Salon, temporarily broad-minded enough to accept it. In fact the scandal caused in 1863 by the deliberate rejection of everything which broke, however mildly, with academic art, and the Emperor's decision to let these rejected paintings figure in a special exhibition – the Salon des Refusés – led to a change of policy by the hanging committee of the official Salon, which two years later admitted not only Manet and Degas, but also Renoir, Pissarro, Berthe Morisot.

So it came about that in the course of 1865–66 Degas got into touch with the independent painters of his generation. But because he was a Parisian, well off, an admirer of Ingres, and inspired by a fresh vision of academic art, he was soon to break away from these men of humbler circumstances who were essentially landscape painters, while he always refused to work in the open air.

The Impressionists formed a group when their Impressionism was still latent and their painting remained more or less traditional, as is easy to realise when one looks at the youthful works of Pissarro, Monet, Renoir, Bazille. They began to move away from one another as soon as their personalities developed.

The Franco-Prussian War of 1870 had a decisive effect on them: Bazille was killed at Beaune-la-Rolande, Sisley ruined; Cézanne went back to Provence; the others attained maturity and a better understanding of the direction they should take. Perhaps too they were unconsciously influenced by that ordeal of self-examination that France passed through after her defeat and the setting up of the Commune in Paris. It is at least certain that the pace of their evolution quickened, and indeed at their first exhibition in 1874 Claude Monet's landscape entitled *Impression* could be taken as representing their aims. These so-called "Impressionist" exhibitions are at the root of the misunderstanding which has treated these strongly individual characters as a group, and even a school. Yet the names of those exhibiting in them should be enough to guard against oversimplification.

These friends whom life was finally to separate were all together at Nadar's, 35, Boulevard des Capucines, on the 15th April, 1874: Cézanne, Degas, Guillaumin, Monet, Berthe Morisot, Pissarro, Renoir and Sisley. With them were two older men who had pointed the way, Boudin and Lépine. But as for the others nobody today would regard them as advanced painters – Félix Bracquemond, Zacharie Astruc, A. F. Attendu, E. Belliard, Edouard Brandon, Cals, Latouche, Lepic, de Nittis, Henri Rouart etc.

The moving spirit in the group was Edgar Degas. Apparently it was he who organized the exhibition. Anyhow it was he who pressed Edouard Manet and that fine engraver Félix Bracquemond to come in with his friends.

A MAN OF SUBSTANCE

Degas was descended from a very old family in Languedoc. His grandfather, Hilaire-René de Gas, was in Paris during the Terror. Warned that government agents were after him, he left hastily for Bordeaux; from there he took ship for Marseilles. There he embarked for Damietta, took part in the Egyptian campaign, then went to Naples with General Championnet. He got married there and became financial adviser to

PORTRAIT OF THE ARTIST WITH A CHARCOAL HOLDER (1854–55)
MUSÉE DU JEU DE PAUME, PARIS

Murat, who was then King of Naples. In 1820 he sold his agency and founded a bank.

Some years later he sent his son Auguste to Paris, to work with his uncle, who had a bank in the Rue de la Tour des Dames, in the Notre-Dame de Lorette district, which was long a haunt of artists – Delacroix had his studio there, while Gustave Moreau's, in the Rue La Rochefoucauld, has since been turned into a museum.

This was the street where Auguste de Gas lived, and from his windows he noticed a young girl newly arrived from America whom he was soon to meet at a friend's house. So it came about that Auguste de Gas, born at Naples, married Célestine Musson, born in New Orleans. They had five children, of whom the eldest, Edgar, was born in Paris, at 8, Rue Saint-Georges on June 19, 1834.

The boy did well at school – the Lycée Louis-Le-Grand. He formed a decided taste for literature, became a respectable Greek and Latin scholar, and won several prizes for drawing. It was planned that he should either follow his father in the family banking business or go into the cotton trade with his mother's brothers in America, and as a beginning he was put to study law.

His father, a lover of music and painting, introduced him to collectors such as Marcille, an old man just like Balzac's Cousin Pons, who took him to the Louvre and showed him the prints in the Bibliothèque Nationale. At the Valpinçons, friends of his father, he came upon some of Ingres' masterpieces, in particular the *Odalisque in a Turban*.

He quickly came to a decision and threw up the law, but when he declared that he was going to devote himself to

HORSEMEN GROUPED IN A LANDSCAPE (c. 1862)
BÜHRLE COLLECTION, ZURICH

painting, his choice was not warmly received at home. To
show his independence, young Edgar hastened to install himself
in an attic and put his name down, in 1853, at the Barrias
studios.

Soon his father, who had lost his wife in 1847, allowed
him to turn one of his rooms in the Rue Mondovi into a

11

studio. He began to work regularly under a pupil of Ingres, Lamothe, in his studio in the Rue du Regard. It was there, says M. P. A. Lemoisne, that he laid the firm basis of that classical technique from which he was later able to venture into more daring experiments. In 1855 he enrolled at the Ecole Nationale des Beaux-Arts, where he was far from industrious.

Ingres' influence showed in his drawings and his first paintings. The year 1855 indeed marked the high tide of Ingres — sixty-eight of his works were on view at the International Exhibition in Paris, and there is no doubt that this collection of a life-time had a deep effect on the young Degas.

Ingres was seventy-five, and since he had been put at the head of the Villa Medici he no longer had a studio at the Ecole des Beaux-Arts. But as soon as he was back in Paris his influence was strongly exerted, and it was all the stronger on Degas because the Valpinçons and Lamothe so often spoke of the great Ingres — he also had the chance of meeting him twice in his studio on the Quai Voltaire.

DISCOVERING ITALY

Family influences were no less decisive. In 1854 his father sent him to make the acquaintance of his relatives in Naples, and this first sight of Italy made him want to return for a longer stay.

Among other activities he had his first lessons in engraving from a friend of his father, the collector, painter, and engraver, Gregorio Soutzo, and long talks with him did much for his development. "Today," he recorded, "I had a fine

12

talk with Monsieur Soutzo. What courage there is in his work – and it's needed! Never compromise with the great order of nature." Yet we shall see that he was to avoid this contact with nature, for the whole of his vast output was conceived in his studio.

This was the period when Degas formed the taste for music which never left him, and he began to go regularly to the Opera.

Soon he was back at Naples, before going on to settle in Rome near Elie Delaunay, where he met the novelist Edmond About, Georges Bizet the composer, Clésinger the sculptor, and the painters Bonnat and Gustave Moreau. Yet it was his stay in Florence and the revelation of the great 15th-century masters which had the decisive effect on him. He used an excellent phrase to express the double trend of his painting: "The secret is to accept what the masters teach you in their works, while creating something different from theirs," an idea repeated in another way with: "Oh, Giotto, let me look at Paris – and Paris, let me look at Giotto!"

He returned to Paris in 1857, and in the following year set off again for Tuscany and Umbria. He was welcomed by his Bellelli aunt and stayed from August, 1858 to April, 1859. There he began on his first great painting to which he was to devote so much time and toil. *Family Portrait* (1859–62) is his largest canvas, one which, after his death, was to prove to the general public that, before being a revolutionary, he was an excellent portrait painter in the classic style. Travelling all over Italy he went back to the beginnings of Western art: "Raphael," he said, "although he is so great, is not the only master. I admire Mantegna and Pollaiuolo as much;

13

THE BELLELLI FAMILY (c. 1860)
MUSÉE DU JEU DE PAUME, PARIS

Ghirlandaio and Botticelli too have aroused deep feelings in me. I shall never forget the famous paintings in Siena nor the half-vanished frescoes in the church at Assisi."

This experience broadened his style, and when Auguste de Gas opened the packing-cases containing the works his son had sent, he wrote to him: "I must say that you have made great progress in your art; the drawing is strong, the colour authentic. You've got rid of that fluid and banal style of drawing, copied from Flandrin [1] and Lamothe, and dropped that dull grey colour. You needn't worry, my dear Edgar: you're on

[1] Hippolyte Flandrin, pupil of Ingres and friend of Lamothe.

STUDY OF HANDS (c. 1862)
MUSÉE DU JEU DE PAUME, PARIS

the right track; you have a great future before you – don't worry, don't be discouraged ... "

Doubtless few fathers have been so far-sighted or so sympathetic; Edgar Degas remained devoted to him all his life – and to his Italian relations to whom he owed much and who welcomed him for long stays in the course of which his character took shape. For he was no longer the industrious pupil of Lamothe; in landscapes and portraits alike, he was both accurate and original. Though not yet sufficiently confident to tackle the great subjects which inspired him, his real character was already apparent in such works as *La Mendiante Romaine.*

But fundamentally it was portraits which interested him; he was beginning to express his determination only to paint what he knew well, and constantly did portraits of himself and his relations, his aunts, his cousins, his grandfather.

Finishing the *Family Portrait,* when he was back in Paris in a studio in the Rue Madame, was the great achievement of this period. Its substantial quality, its draughtmanship, the freshness of its composition, all make it worthy to hang in the Jeu de Paume beside Manet's *Picnic* and Claude Monet's *Women in a Garden.*

THE HISTORICAL PAINTER

This picture of the Bellelli family, in their home setting, represents a stage in Degas' evolution. After the years taken up with this huge canvas and with portraits of Monsieur and Madame Valpinçon, of Ruelle, and of Bonnat, he felt ready

16

to begin a different sort of painting, of which he had seen so many striking examples in Italy – history painting, which called up great events to stimulate the imagination.

Our own ideas are so remote from those of Degas at this period of his life that this side of his work has become somewhat alien to us. Having given up so much time to the accurate portrayal of faces familiar to him, he sought out subjects in ancient Greece and in the Middle Ages. While he agreed with Théophile Gautier that history painting combined "thought, style and composition," he realised that it had been reduced to the lowest academic level. He too believed that "the day of its disappearance would mean a great loss to art" and felt that he had the power to revive it. So he devoted years to numbers of drawings, plans, and sketches. Five paintings emerged from all these attempts: *Young Spartan Girls Challenging Boys at Wrestling* (1860); *Semiramis Building a Town* (1861); *Alexander and Bucephalus* (there are two versions of this); *Jephtha's Daughter* and *Disasters of Orleans* (1865).

Degas' style is already apparent in these curious works. First the mysterious atmosphere which envelopes them marks them off from all the pictures on similar themes annually shown at the Salon. Moreover Degas' Spartan girls look much more like the little Montmartre girls who posed for him than young Greeks. In all of them a prejudice in favour of stylised treatment reveals the strength of Ingres' influence on him.

Yet with *Jephtha's Daughter* it is obvious that Degas had Delacroix in mind – he even made a note on one sketch: "For the red of Jephtha's robe, remember the orange-red shades in Delacroix, old man ..." For he admired the Delacroix of

PORTRAIT OF A YOUNG WOMAN (c. 1867)
MUSÉE DU JEU DE PAUME, PARIS

The Crusaders' Entry no less than the Ingres of *The Turkish Bath*.

These paintings, which are only academic on the surface, emphasize the young painter's determination to react against the ideas of his age: unaffected by Edouard Manet's experiments, he withstood the influence which such writers as Zola, the Goncourts, and Duranty were exerting on advanced painters.

THE PAINTER OF MODERN LIFE

Yet a moment came when he had to realise that it is impossible to hold aloof from the times in which one lives, that all such attempts are doomed – understood neither by the academics, who saw him getting essentially plastic effects out of classical themes, nor by the independents, who worked direct from nature. Perhaps too he sensed that his technique, highly developed though it already was, was hardly equal to such complex paintings, and he bowed to the golden rule of all great masters: to belong to one's age, without yielding to passing fads. He found a phrase to express his submission: "Two centuries ago I would have painted Suzannah bathing, and now I paint women in hip baths."

Duranty's direct influence marked his fresh development around 1865, for the author of *Le Malheur d'Henriette Gérard* had openly declared: "Three centuries of false education in the arts are responsible for the impotence of contemporary art; people have drawn back from their own age, thinking that they have a better idea of the past which they've never seen than of the present in which they live and

19

MEMBERS OF THE ORCHESTRA (c. 1868–69)
MUSÉE DU JEU DE PAUME, PARIS

PORTRAIT OF MLLE. DIHAU AT THE PIANO (1868–70)
MUSÉE DU JEU DE PAUME, PARIS   21

move and have their being, and such people must answer for their own lack of intelligence." Like all controversialists, Duranty was very unfair and, though he paid tribute to Courbet, he forgot that his age had produced Millet's and Daumier's masterpieces, Delacroix's *Freedom on the Barricades,* and that Manet was already adding his name to those of many painters "truly representative of their age."

Degas first met Edouard Manet at the Louvre. If their characters are often set together, it is obvious that they were related in their identical conception of art, no less than in the fact of belonging to the same rank of society. Both were inspired by the idea of reconciling classicism and life, museum art and truth to reality. So Degas invited Manet to his father's musical evenings, while Manet in turn introduced his new friend to the Café Guerbois.

Degas was by nature a misanthropist. But when he made an effort to conquer his reserve, he could be very good company. Evenings at the Café Guerbois had an excellent effect on him because they tore him away from his fanatical toil in his studio, where he strove bitterly to analyse the faces of his models. These artistic discussions – so fruitless when they only result in abstract theorizing – were obviously useful to an artist who was always inclined to remain shut up inside himself.

THE PORTRAIT PAINTER

He chose portraits as a means of escape from that academic art on which he had at last decided to turn his back for ever. Perhaps he still did not feel mature enough to embark on the study of scenes in real life, though he was drawn to observe

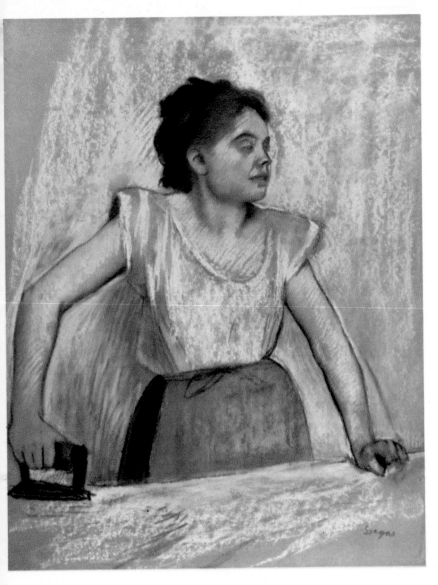

WOMAN IRONING (1869)
MUSÉE DU JEU DE PAUME, PARIS

attitudes and expressions; at the same time he worked furiously on more and more poses which for him were always "a pitiless struggle between a painter and his model."

In the years before 1870, he painted some fifty portraits, and those who sat for them were always people known to him, for he tried hard to catch a resemblance in their familiar features and to bring out their real character no less than their appearance. Gradually abandoning observation of the face alone, he tried, as he has recorded in one of his notebooks, to portray people in typical and familiar attitudes, above all to give one and the same expression to the face and to the whole figure. In his desire to represent real life, he attached an ever growing importance to the circumstances and background of his models, and so prepared himself to get outside his studio and the setting to which his canvases were still confined.

*

It is all the more exciting to follow this slow development because Edgar Degas had already begun on those experiments in lighting, composition, and technique which he was to follow all his life. One might even say that his artistic character took its final form in the course of these prolonged meditations on the human face. Already a great freedom is apparent in the portrait of Hortense Valpinçon which shows the child leaning for a moment on the corner of a table as she finishes biting an apple. The care he gave to the carpet, the thick fabric, the hangings on the wall, the little girl's clothes is prophetic of the same care which Edouard Vuillard was one day to lavish on capturing such moments.

In the course of visits to the country or the seaside, Degas also dashed off landscapes startling in their exactitude. This was also the period of *The Injured Jockey*, a remarkable piece of work, somewhat awkwardly managed, yet promising the boldness of treatment that was to come. Then at last he showed what he was later to do with studies of ballet girls when he exhibited, in the Salon of 1868, *Mlle. Fiocre dans le Ballet "La Source."*

THE PAINTER OF WOMEN

The importance of his work as a portrait painter should not be allowed to overshadow the experiments which he was then making in other directions. Several canvases showed the path he was going to take. This man who only painted what he knew really well was being drawn into an analysis of the female body which was constantly intensified.

All his life he was to paint women: a well-off woman sitting for her portrait, a girl dancing on the stage at the Opera, a model washing or undressing; yet he had always been suspicious of women, never allowing them into his life and, a confirmed bachelor, only letting the plainest women act as his housekeepers: "He came to sit beside me," Berthe Morisot once recorded, "and pretended that he was going to make love to me. But this turned out to be nothing but a long dissertation on the proverbs of Solomon and the effect of a brawling woman on a wise man..."

It would be a great mistake to see in Degas one of those painters who have been crossed by fate. The most that could be said is that he was his own worst enemy, for he was rich, intelligent and cultured, a witty and sardonic talker, warmly welcomed among the writers and musicians whose company

PORTRAIT OF JEANTAUD, LINÉ AND LAINÉ (MARCH, 1871)
MUSÉE DU JEU DE PAUME, PARIS

27

◁ PAGANS THE GUITAR PLAYER AND AUGUSTE DE GAS (c. 1870)
MUSÉE DU JEU DE PAUME, PARIS

he preferred to that of the independent painters with whom posterity has linked his name. On the contrary, he liked to sit down to a meal at a restaurant in the Rue Notre-Dame de Lorette with such academic painters as Gervex, Cormon, Humbert, Gérome, and Forain, with whom he was as friendly as with the sculptor Bartholomé, though that did not prevent his saying of him: "He paints with his hands in my pockets."

His phrases went the rounds of drawing-rooms and cafés: "They move under our own steam," he said, when he saw academic painters borrowing from the independents; and "they knock us down and then ransack our pockets." When he saw Bastien-Lepage's *Lovers,* he said, "They're making love behind Pissarro's back." He called Boldini "an engine-driver's Watteau" and Albert Besnard "one of the old school pretending to be a schoolboy"; as for Gustave Moreau, he was "a hermit who knew the times of trains."

No wonder that Bonnat once said: "I keep out of Degas' way, for talking with him makes me fed up with my painting for a week." Anyhow he preferred the people he met at his father's Mondays to artists, people who cared for music, singers and instrumentalists, such as Dilhau, the bassoon player who was to introduce him to the dancers at the Opera.

He went often to the opera hall in the Rue Le Peletier and then, when it was burnt down, to Garnier's Opera. The paintings of classical ballet he made taught us that here was a form of pure beauty, austere, governed by stringent rules, in which delicacy softened a geometric precision. It was he who enabled us to grasp André Levinson's teaching, when he tried to make us see the elegant perfection of movement in a Pavlova Zambelli, Lorciat or Chauviré.

When the war of 1870 broke out, Degas volunteered for an artillery battery which was defending Paris. There he came upon an old school friend from Louis-le-Grand, Henri Rouart, and renewed a friendship which was to last without a break for the rest of his life.

The war made so sharp a dividing line that it is possible to place the real beginnings of Impressionism in the years 1870–71. For Degas, portraits were no longer the chief interest, and *The Opera Orchestra,* painted about 1868, had shown the direction in which he was to develop. *The Ballet of "Robert the Devil"* of 1872 sets in the foreground a row of stalls, then the Opera orchestra, while the background consists of an architectural design which shows off the dancers.

This same year, 1872, marked the beginning of his series of ballet girls, studies observed either on the stage or in the course of rehearsals. *The Dancer's Greenroom at the Opera in the Rue Le Peletier* already displays one of those moments which Degas spent his life in trying to recapture. His later interest in photography evidently originated in his desire to seize the perfect but transient gesture which had caught his observant eye.

At this time he was going to race-courses even more readily and more often than to the Opera. *Before the Grandstand* and *False Start* were the first of a long series, the work of a painter who could not work until he had soaked himself in his subject and who, like Daumier, confined himself to a limited number of themes, yet was constantly able to endow them with fresh interest.

HENRI VALPINÇON IN CHILDHOOD (1870)
PRIVATE COLLECTION, PARIS

DISCOVERING AMERICA

It was also in 1872 that he visited the United States: his
brother René, who had been with his uncle in the cotton
trade in New Orleans, came to Paris and suggested taking
Edgar to America; but, though he had so much family feeling,
he was already a stay-at-home, and it was only at the last

moment that he agreed to embark on the *Scotia*. His stay in Louisiana was to stimulate Degas to a number of works, two large pastels, and portraits such as the *Woman with a Jar* in the Louvre, but only one of these pictures shows the atmosphere of a country which was foreign to him – his study of a half-naked coloured woman, a quadroon. Even *The Cotton Exchange in New Orleans* might have been painted by him in France. This masterpiece, which shows a return to a smooth technique and meticulous drawing, is quite distinct from his studies of dancers in which he seems to have borrowed from his Impressionist friends something of their skill in order to bring out the artificial atmosphere of the theatre.

On November 27 he wrote a long letter to Lorentz Frölich, the Danish painter whom he had met at Manet's, which is worth quoting: "I have seen much that's new, which has given me a number of ideas, my dear Frölich. But already I'm setting them aside, as I only want to get back to my own place and devote myself to that. Art is not an enlargement, but a concentration. And if you insist on an image of what I mean, I would say that if one wants to produce the finest fruits one has to train oneself against the wall like a fruit-tree – spend one's life there, arms outstretched and open-mouthed to take in and digest everything that passes by, everything that's close at hand, and live simply on that ... I've accumulated a mass of ideas which would need ten life-times to carry out – but in another six weeks I'll throw them all up without a sigh, just to be back home and never go away again."

"Art is not an enlargement, but a concentration." Degas summed up his whole ambition in this phrase. This was his

31

THREE DANCERS AT PRACTICE (1873)
PRIVATE COLLECTION, PARIS

artistic and aesthetic creed, and in future nothing was to divert him from it, for as Paul Valéry said: "Degas is one of those men who only care for what really matters."

His letters from New Orleans include some in which he shows himself with least reserve. Taking up some ideas already mentioned to Frölich, he wrote to Henri Rouart: "One only cares about and gives artistic expression to things which have become a part of oneself. Novelties are first attractive, then boring. I admire many things here," he added, "but I won't be sorry to see the last of them. Life is too short, and one only has just the strength needed for it. I want to get home and settle down to an orderly existence." Yet there is a curious regret in the lines that follow: "I do want to settle down. I wouldn't even object to the right woman in this new sort of existence I have in mind – even a few children of my own wouldn't be out of the way. I dream of something complete and well organized – in the style of Poussin, or Corot in his old age. It's the right moment for it. If it doesn't materialize, life will be the same, but less enjoyable, less solid – and filled with regrets." It is odd that a man so reserved should at times be so frank in his letters. He not only told Frölich that there ought to be a distinction between art in Paris and in Louisiana, but added words which in their emotional tone contradict that surliness of disposition that Degas seems to have been at such pains to keep up: "I've read through my letter, and it's very unresponsive compared with yours – don't hold it against me!"

This letter has to be set beside a very moving one to his friend de Valernes, though written twenty years later in 1890: "I'm writing to ask you to forgive me for something which crops up often in our talk – and more often in your mind:

33

the fact that, in the course of our long artistic association, I have been, or seemed to be, hard on you. I have always been very hard on myself ... I have been, or seemed to be, hard on everybody – driven into a roughness which really rose out of my uncertainties and irritability. I seemed to myself so badly put together, so ill-equipped and weak, although my ideas on art appeared to me sound enough. I sulked with everybody, especially with myself. Please forgive me if – owing to this confounded art – I have given offence to the great distinction and intelligence which I know you have, perhaps even to your feelings." No admission could be clearer nor more heart-rending, coming from an artist who certainly carried his reserve too far.

DEVOTION TO ART

In the year 1872, to which we must now return, not only did Degas reach maturity in his art, but he also settled down to the sort of life that he had outlined to Henri Rouart – in future very little travelling or visits to the country, nothing but devotion to his work, a devotion which was even more intense because he had begun to fear for his eyesight. All his life he was to have trouble with his eyes and indeed to end by going almost blind. Before such a disaster happened he had then to accomplish the work he had in mind and say what he had to say, without making concessions to anybody or anything.

Back in his studio at the Rue Blanche in March, 1873, Edgar Degas was no longer quite the same man who had set out for Louisiana five months before. His ideas on art and life had grown clearer in the course of his travels; he had reached the

35

36   DANCING CLASS (1874)
MUSÉE DU JEU DE PAUME, PARIS

DANCER ON THE STAGE (c. 1876) ▷
MUSÉE DU JEU DE PAUME, PARIS

fullness of maturity and was never again to turn aside from the path he had marked out.

Giving up any idea of a compromise between academic art and what was not yet known as "the art of our own age" – a compromise that was anyhow out of the question – he settled down to observe. But he was far from indiscriminate in this, for two subjects held his real attention: women and horses. He never tired of contemplating the play of muscles under a woman's skin or under a thoroughbred's glossy coat, and he tried hard to capture those movements which best brought out his own often very personal conception of beauty.

This fundamental change, which was the effect of an inner development which had been going on for a long time, only came out on his return from America, and it was so marked that this visit may be considered as beginning for him a new conception both of his art and his life.

First of all he made a complete break with the official Salon where he had exhibited up to 1870 – and there was nothing to stop him exhibiting there again, as did Edouard Manet, more or less successfully; the subjects he went in for were, at least superficially, familiar to those who frequented this great artistic occasion, the only one that took place regularly every year. For the future he declared: "The realist movement no longer needs to compete with others. It already exists in its own right and it should have a place of its own. There must be a Salon especially for realists."

Yet in these words the seeds of future trouble with the Impressionists are already visible. It is true that this term was not yet in use – but Claude Monet and his friends wanted to record their "impressions" whereas Degas wanted to be a "realist" both in choice of subject and in technique. Today it is evident that from the beginning there was a misunderstanding between the organizer of the 1874 exhibition and those who exhibited their work with his.

Another factor, a material one, served to mark Degas off from the Impressionists: nearly all of them were poor and permanently obsessed with the need to raise a few francs to support their families, while Degas, who belonged to a family that was well off, already had his devoted admirers, such as Faure, the singer, who in 1874 paid five thousand francs – the equivalant of over fifteen hundred pounds in money today – for *The Dance Examination*.

So it came about that in 1875 Degas was in a position to come to the help of his brother Achille whose business was on its last legs and to undertake the support of the whole family. It is true that he made no concessions in his art, but his subjects – the theatre and racing – happened to be popular; of all those who exhibited at the "Salon Nadar" he was the one most kindly treated by the critics, and he was never at a loss for purchasers.

That did not prevent his making constant requests for money from Durand-Ruel, his dealer. There is not a letter to him, in the series from 1883 to 1908, which does not contain some such demand. Yet this was the time when Degas was acquiring the magnificent collection of masterpieces which were found in his home after his death, and he sometimes paid a lot for them – although when he was on holiday with the Valpinçons in the summer of 1884, he wrote to his dealer: "My housekeeper brought me a tax demand this morning ... fifty francs will be enough, but if you can give her a hundred, there will be some left for her." Requests for two hundred or five hundred francs follow one another on various occasions. He was still complaining on August 10, 1904: "I have bitter thoughts about art when I consider that I've reached old age without ever making money."

It is beside the point to enquire whether he was poor or miserly, for he never held back when it was a matter of buying some painting, drawing, or engraving that he really wanted. If he had carried out his plan of leaving a museum

RACE-COURSE, BY THE GRANDSTAND (1879)
MUSÉE DU JEU DE PAUME, PARIS

WOMAN AT A WINDOW (c. 1878)
COURTAULD INSTITUTE, LONDON

given over to his collections and his own works, we would have one of the finest galleries imaginable. His room in the Rue Victor Massé contained Delacroix's sketch for *The Battle of Nancy,* two Corots painted in Italy, two Manets, many Ingres drawings and water colours, and others by Delacroix, Puvis de Chavannes, and Suzanne Valadon, who had been his model and whom he had encouraged in her painting.

In his drawing-room there was Manet's *Blue Sofa,* an Ingres study for *Jupiter and Thetis,* a Corot landscape. In the hall there was Gauguin's copy of Manet's *Olympia.* He also had works by El Greco, Goya, Cuyp, Daumier's *Seated Man,* as well as Renoirs, Van Goghs, Cézannes, Pissarros, Sisleys; paintings and engravings by his favourite Japanese, in particular Kiyonaga's *Bathing.* But it was chiefly Ingres and Delacroix who stood out – as they had always been outstanding to him: there were twenty paintings and thirty-three drawings by Ingres, while Delacroix was represented by a copy of the Rubens in the Medici Gallery, an *Entombment of Christ,* a portrait of Baron de Schwitzer and some sixty sketches. As for the engravings, they could hardly be counted, for he had no less than eighteen hundred Daumiers and two thousand lithographs by Gavarni!

THE LAST OF THE IMPRESSIONIST EXHIBITIONS

The 1876 exhibition at Durand-Ruel's 11, Rue Le Peletier had brought together the most famous of the "Salon Nadar" group and could still support the illusion that the Impressionists were indeed a group. With Degas there was Monet,

TWO DANCERS ON THE STAGE (c. 1877)
COURTAULD INSTITUTE, LONDON ▷

Bazille – his work was posthumously exhibited – Berthe Morisot, Renoir, Pissarro, Sisley – but also Caillebotte, Beneau, Cals, Desboutin, Jacques François, Alphonse Legros, Levert, Lepic, Jean-Baptiste Millet, A. A. Ottin, Henri Rouart, and Tillot. In April 1877, Cézanne, Degas, Guillaumin, Monet, Pissarro, Renoir, and Sisley exhibited for the third time, with several newcomers such as Cordey, Lamy, Maureau.

Among those who took part in the fourth exhibition, in April and May 1879, are: Bracquemond and his wife, Caillebotte, Cals, Mary Cassatt, Degas, Forain, Lebourg, Monet, Pissarro, Piette, Rouart, Henri Somm, Tillot and Zandomeneghi. A letter from Degas to Félix Bracquemond tells us that this exhibition was enough of a success for each exhibitor to receive 439 francs, fifty centimes – "which is quite good," he adds.

Yet already Renoir, Cézanne and Sisley had dropped out. Claude Monet no longer appeared in 1880, the year in which Gauguin's name first figured. Those who took part in this fifth exhibition were Monsieur and Madame Bracquemond, Caillebotte, Mary Cassatt, Degas, Forain, Gauguin, Guillaumin, Lebourg, Levert, Berthe Morisot, Pissarro, Raffaëlli, Rouart, Tillot, Vidal, Vignon, Zandomeneghi – and more or less the same names recurred in 1881.

THE SCULPTOR

At this 1881 exhibition Degas showed his first piece of sculpture, the *Fourteen-year-old Dancing Girl* which Paul Mantz described in these terms: "The wretched child is standing up in a cheap muslin dress. She's at work, bowed, already a little tired. Her face, or rather her small snout, sticks out, shameless as an animal's. Monsieur Degas is merciless. If he goes on with sculpture in this style, his name will be listed among the cruellest of artists."

Degas persevered and he has a place in the history of sculpture, for Robert Rey comes near to claiming that the two men of genius in sculpture at the end of the 19th century and the beginning of the 20th were Rodin and Degas. The seventy-five works he has left us fully support this opinion. They are chiefly nude studies, but include several horses and some ballet girls. Yet many of those that he started have been lost, either because he dropped them, because they crumbled away in his studio, or because he destroyed them before he had finished them. Those that we have were mostly found after his death and cast in bronze by Hébrard.

It has been said that Degas turned so much to sculpture towards the end of his life because, with his failing eyesight, modelling was easier than painting for him. The truth is that from the beginning of his career he was torn between the two arts. During his first stay in Rome he wrote to Pierre Cornu: "I often wonder whether I'll be a painter or a sculptor. I'll confess to you that I'm very perplexed on this point." His perplexity is not surprising when one studies his drawing which has all the qualities of a sculptor's. Moreover, in the works of his last period which summed up the results of so many experiments, it is obvious that form was much more important to the artist than colour.

Then again it was impossible that a man so interested in all the problems of technique and in experiments with painting,

drawing, and engraving should neglect clay and wax modelling. His letters offer stimulating details about his work on the bust of Hortense Valpinçon in 1884, when he wrote: "I have begun on a large bust, to include the arms, working in clay mixed with small pebbles." It is a pity that he did not finish this attempt in a medium which he was apparently using for the first and last time.

THE SOLITARY

The last exhibition of the Impressionists – or as Degas would have preferred to call them, the Independents – took place in 1886. Degas' uncompromising character, his determination to keep some painters out and bring others in, contributed not a little to the breaking up of a group whose unity, as shown above, was more superficial than real. In future he went his austere way alone, equally scornful of approval from advanced or academic circles. The latter, by turning down Manet and Degas, lost an unexpected opportunity to make good the mistake of their predecessors who, prompted by the disciples of Ingres, had rejected first of all Delacroix and Géricault, and then the painters of the Barbizon school.

If the division between art and official institutions had been less complete, Degas would never have joined a group of artists with whom he really had little in common. He was always sarcastic about landscape painters who could only paint from nature, and his harsh opinions on some of those taking part in the Impressionist exhibitions are well known – his attitude was at times so offensive that he ended by being

47

DANCER IN HER DRESSING ROOM (c. 1879)
OSKAR REINHART COLLECTION, WINTERTHUR

AT THE STOCK EXCHANGE (C. 1879)
MUSÉE DU JEU DE PAUME, PARIS

THE MEET.
BÜHRLE COLLECTION, ZURICH

one of the few survivors from the first group to exhibit. On the other hand he was on friendly terms with Elie Delaunay, Léon Bonnat, Gustave Moreau, Paul Dubois, Bartholomé and other masters from the Academy or the official Salon.

This double rôle of classical and modern painter is far from being the only paradox in the life and work of Edgar Degas. There is no character more reserved, nor more disturbing among those who made the second half of the 19th century one of the greatest artistic periods of all time.

Apart from the near-blindness which cast a tragic shadow over his last years, it is useless to look in Degas' life for those extraordinary features which, from Van Gogh to Utrillo, from Gauguin to Modigliani, have led some to believe in a tragic destiny hanging over the heads of the greatest modern painters. We know nothing of the intimate details of his life, beyond what he tells us himself in his work, in a few confidences to close friends, or in his letters. Even in these he keeps up a reserve which offers nothing to explain the deep-rooted causes of his misanthropic outlook. Painting was his life – he lived for nothing else – and he was never satisfied, constantly retouching his canvases, overloading them, destroying them; he was at the opposite pole from most friends of his youth who – apart from Cézanne – produced great works as naturally as a tree bears fruit.

He rejected anything which might keep him from his work; and love was the first victim of this resolution. Ambroise Vollard who, whatever may be said on the other side, was in the best position to understand him records this curious remark: "Vollard, you should get married. You don't know what loneliness is like when you grow old." But when the dealer asked him why he had remained a bachelor, he hastened to add: "I was too much afraid of hearing my wife say, when I had finished a painting: 'That's a pretty picture you've done ...'"

It was seldom that he spoke so openly. What came out most often, in talk and writing, was his perpetual dissatisfaction. He was far from being as sure of himself as he let people imagine; and from this came his reluctance to sell his canvases in the hope that, so long as he kept and worked on them, he would be able to bring them closer to the impossible ideal that he had set before him.

Once when it was a question of having his fine sculpture cast in bronze, he replied: "It's too much of a responsibility to let anything in bronze survive one – that's stuff that lasts for ever."

He gave himself away again when he said with assumed irony: "It's lucky that I haven't yet found my style – that would be a real nuisance."

THEMES AND VARIATIONS

Degas finally took to heart, around 1875, the advice that Duranty had been constantly giving him over the years. He set himself to notice the scenes of everyday life around him, in the street, cafés, and race-courses.

First he had given up mythological subjects in favour of portraits. Then he had begun to group musicians or dancers on his canvas. Now he turned to paintings which might be said to "tell a story" if problems of composition were not always his chief concern. The details of his subjects are so exact that his double portrait of Ellen André and Marcellin Desboutin

DANCERS ON THE STAGE: "LE PAS BATTU" (c. 1879)
BÜHRLE COLLECTION, ZURICH

has received the title of *Absinthe;* while the disturbing scene which shows a man standing and looking at a woman in tears has been given the name of *Rape.*

52

BEFORE THE START (c. 1878–80)
BÜHRLE COLLECTION, ZURICH

But it is the subtle blending of whites and greys which attracts us in *The Chiropodist*, in the Camondo Collection, and it is of small significance that the pictures he painted at this time are called *Sulking, Amateur Jockeys by a Carriage, Melancholy, Women Ironing, Women Carrying Laundry:* these are only concessions to the taste of the age which in no way conflict with his experiments in composition, in organizing forms, or in contrasting and blending colours, which attract us far more today than the "story" which the painter also has to tell us.

53

Even the portraits that Degas went on painting became constantly less important to him than the picture itself, which enabled him to vary the composition – an apparent detail often counted more than the model's face.

But it was the world of the theatre which held a special attraction for him. When he had been working all day in his studio, he felt the need to immerse himself in an atmosphere alive with noise and colour. He went to the Opera more than ever, behind the scenes and into the greenroom. But he went as often to the music-hall; at the Eldorado he saw and applauded Térésa, and the music-halls of the Champs-Elysées inspired some of his most intense and complex works. Among them are *The Ambassadors Music-hall* of 1876, *Woman Singer with a Glove,* and *The Dog's Song,* in which a music-hall star imitated a poodle begging. He loved clowns and whimsical English acts. He painted a girl acrobat at the Fernando Circus, *Miss Lola.*

For the three groups of subjects to which he had confined himself almost exclusively – portraits, stage scenes, race-courses – he used every sort of technique: crayon, black-lead pencil, charcoal, black-lead heightened with chalk, pastel, gouache, sometimes oil. As for the paper he used, his friends record that its strength, texture, and tint were deliberately chosen every time for the purpose he had in view.

But it was from pastel, no less than oil, that he drew his subtlest and most characteristic effects. Eighteenth-century portrait painters had so abused this medium that since their time artists had been inclined to neglect a process which was thought to be lacking in firmness. Manet made use of it from time to time, but Degas was to find in it the ideal medium for bringing out the artificial gleam of light playing over a dancer's dress, or for catching some transient impression, and he often finished in pastel a drawing that he had begun in charcoal. He even used it at times to heighten his monotypes, and he was unique in his ability to draw from these the subtle effects which have been so much admired.

Yet it has to be said that it was classical dancing which most gave him the sustenance of which he stood in need. First

THE "BALLET DE L'AFRICAINE" (1879)
PRIVATE COLLECTION

of all there was the female body which he still refrained from subjecting to a naked analysis; then there was the intense physical effort required to triumph over the laws of gravity; there was the sharp exactitude of an art which rejected all compromise and called for mathematical precision; finally there was all the fascination of dancing, the picturesque life behind the scenes, the thousand and one details which he was able to observe at dancing classes: he displays the ballet girl to us, enchanting on the stage a moment ago, now slouched on a bench beside her mother, Madame Cardinal; then the girl practising with her hand on the rail, putting on her ballet shoe, resting in her dressing-room, going on the stage, dancing either in her great moment alone or together with the others ... There was no end to the opportunities that the Opera presented to Degas in a period of over thirty years: paintings, drawings, pastels, monotypes, sculpture.

But the more progress he made in this vast work, the more he drew away from the experiments of his contemporaries – not that he was opposed to the great revolution brought about by the friends he had known at the Café Guerbois and the Nouvelle-Athènes. But their problems were very different from those of an artist who was above all looking for a sense of direction.

INFLUENCES ON DEGAS

The Japanese helped him to find this sense of direction, as austere as Cézanne's, but very different from his. It is the fashion nowadays to speak with some scorn of the engravings which disclosed this art to writers and artists in the last years of the 19th century. Today people go back to the originals,

BALLET SCENE (c. 1880)
PRIVATE COLLECTION (FORMERLY VALLOTTON COLLECTION, LAUSANNE)

the paintings which inspired these popular engravers who are
readily placed on a level with the print-sellers of Epinal.
Their quantity has considerably lowered their cost, but not
their artistic value, which is still of some importance.

Anyhow these engravings came as an amazing revelation at the time when Bracquemond or the Goncourts discovered them at Bing's and Madame Desoye's and introduced them to the Impressionists and their friends. Without their influence the work of Gauguin and Van Gogh would not have been the same. As for Degas, what struck him most about the Japanese was the boldness of their composition, their discoveries in the field of perspective which had seemed to have been settled once and for all by the Renaissance.

It is necessary to borrow the language of the cinema to explain Degas' experiments: close-ups and long shots, "pans" and "tilts," mid-long shots and mid-close shots – these technical expressions are surely the most suitable to apply to the composition of Degas' most original works, especially in the last phase of his life, in the astounding series of pastels in which he tried hard to capture those attitudes which would best bring out the play of a woman's muscles – when her body became for him an excuse for an almost abstract combination of forms.

Everything contributes some element to form a character as complex as Degas: Ingres had taught him the plastic value of the distortions which this "classical" painter had imposed on his Turkish girls bathing or his Thetis at the feet of Jupiter; what such painters as Outamaro, Hiroshige and Hokusai gave him has just been noted above; it was to Duranty that he owed the attention he paid to scenes of daily life – and Edmond de Goncourt, recording in his journal a visit to his studio in 1874, remarked on the resemblance between himself and the painter he had just discovered:

"His choice has fallen on laundresses and ballet girls. I can

WOMAN DOING HER HAIR (1880–85)
MUSÉE DU JEU DE PAUME, PARIS ▷

have nothing to say against this choice since, in my *Manette Salomon*, I have celebrated these two trades as offering the most picturesque models of women in our own age." It is true that Degas painted women ironing or washing clothes in preference to other Parisian working women. He thought so much of them during his stay in New Orleans that, having described to Henri Rouart "the exquisite Indian women," he exclaimed: "And I'm all for our exquisite French laundering!"

Goncourt's opinion of Degas is a strange one. Yet it may not be so wrong to see in him a man who was "morbid, neurotic, with a vision so inflamed that he was afraid of losing his eyesight, but for that very reason sensitive in the extreme and reacting forcibly to everything." Finally: "For me he is the man who so far has been best able to catch the inner spirit of modern life in the image presented to us. But will he ever accomplish something really perfect? I don't know. It seems to me that his mind is full of anxieties."

Stéphane Mallarmé is another writer whose relations with Degas would be interesting to know in detail. It is not easy to say whether he had any influence on his painting, but it is obvious that his example was largely responsible for the series of sonnets published after Degas' death. There is an echo of Mallarmé in this quatrain:

> This fountain that's reborn,
> A formal garden's pride,
> Lives with us though forlorn
> As a heart crucified.

Poetry seemed moreover to be an art even more difficult than painting to Degas:

"What a trade!" he said to Mallarmé. "I've wasted a day

over this damned sonnet without getting a step further. Yet I've no lack of ideas. I've too many ..."

"Yes," answered the poet. "But it's words, not ideas, that go to the making of sonnets!"

DEGAS AND LAUTREC

Only one painter of his age really had anything in common with Degas – Toulouse-Lautrec, who was thirty years younger. Yet everything about this aristocrat, who in his deformity had whole-heartedly given himself up to painting and debauchery, was of a character to set him apart from the middle-class – and misanthropic – nature of Edgar Degas.

But it is obvious that the two of them were closely related in their conception of art. Both had taken a long time to draw away from academic ideas, both detested nature, both looked in the same places for their subjects – theatres, race-courses, music-halls, bawdy houses; both were responsible for the most perceptive portraits made towards the close of the 19th century.

They were unique among the great painters of their age in seeing beyond the surface of the human face, exposing its intimate secrets and offering them to our gaze.

It is a pity that Degas' character did not allow of the closer association that Lautrec desired. He had a deep admiration for the older man; he was constantly studying his work, and there is little doubt that his own was directly inspired by it. It is true that their technique had nothing in common, but the spirit of their work and their resolve to be "painters of modern life" should have brought them together, and it is not

61

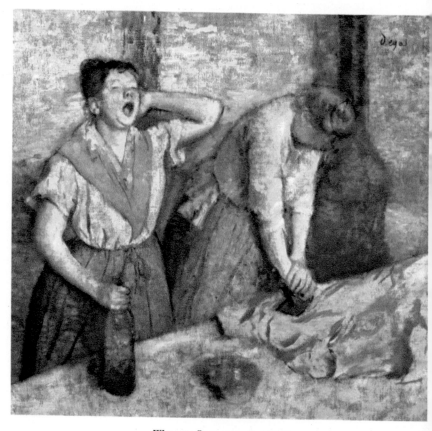

WOMEN IRONING (c. 1884)
MUSÉE DU JEU DE PAUME, PARIS

BALLET GIRL DRESSING (c. 1889) ▷
BÜHRLE COLLECTION, ZURICH

quite out of the question to speculate whether Degas' influence on those round him might not have saved Lautrec from the depths which closed over him.

It is difficult to make out just what Degas thought of him. He seems to have been irritated by an art which must have appeared to him as a sort of caricature of his own. Yet one evening up at Montmartre he said to him: "I've just come from Durand-Ruel's, where I was shown some things of yours. They're very fine. There's a real expression of character in them. I congratulate you. I was delighted to see them."

Overwhelmed by this unexpected praise, Lautrec asked Anquetin who was with him whether he thought that it was seriously meant. Whereupon Anquetin had to reply: "Surely you could see that he was pulling your leg!"

Lautrec sometimes had an opportunity of meeting the older man at the Dilhaus' house. They had Degas' painting *Members of the Orchestra* which Lautrec admired so much that one evening, after a dinner to which he had invited the Natanson brothers and some friends, he took them without warning to the Dilhaus and into the room where this picture was, exclaiming: "That's the last course of the meal!"

It was the Dilhaus who gave him one of the last pleasures in his life when they had him to dinner with Degas in the spring of 1900, after Lautrec had been shut up for some months in the asylum at Neuilly. Thadée Natanson has recorded that Lautrec showed a real deference towards Degas, while with others – even those he admired – he seemed hardly to know the meaning of the word.

One other person formed a transient link between these two men who were so dissimilar but equally eccentric – Suzanne

Valadon. Having long been Lautrec's model and mistress, she went over to Degas though with less sensational results. Yet Degas realised better than Lautrec that the drawings which the woman who was known as "Maria the Terrible" dashed off between a couple of poses showed proof of the great painter that she was to become.

THE MAN AND HIS WORK

Details of Degas' life in middle and old age are to be found in the testimony of his friends and above all in his letters, which tell of his various moves and at the same time reveal some of his characteristics.

There is also plenty of evidence on his method of work. In 1882 he is recorded as asking his friend Hecht to get him permission to attend the dancing examination at the Opera. This is a surprising request, especially when he adds: "I've painted so many dance examinations without ever having seen one that I'm a little ashamed of myself." His visual memory has so often been praised, but perhaps his greatest gift was his imagination.

In the same year he went to Switzerland, and from there sent some odd aphorisms to his friend Bartholomé:

"The definition of love is to shoot with the eyes bandaged."

"'Why should I travel?' said a station-master."

After days in his studio immersed in work, he was reluctant to go out for walks in the Paris he so loved, and he confided, again to Bartholomé: "Now that the days are getting longer,

GETTING OUT OF THE BATH (c. 1889–90)
JOSEPH MÜLLER COLLECTION, SOLEURE

I have to force myself only to spend half the day in my studio."

It was to the same friend that he confided his melancholy reflections and surrendered to his ingrained pessimism: "Ah, the days are gone when I was sure of my strength, clear-headed and full of plans. Now I'm quickly going downhill, to roll heaven knows where, wrapped up – as though in brown paper – in a bundle of wretched pastels." And to Henri Lerolle he wrote: "If you were a bachelor, just turned fifty, you would know these moments when you lock the door on yourself, not only against your friends. You get rid of everything, and once you're alone you tear yourself to pieces, to die simply of disgust."

These moments of despair were only phases which did not prevent his getting through the work to which he was so bitterly devoted. There were too moments of relief which came as unexpectedly as his periods of depression. In one of his visits to the Valpinçons at Ménil-Hubert he admitted, almost regretfully, to Henri Rouart: "I'm not really bad at heart." But in another letter he amended this to say: "I'm not really warm-hearted, and family and other troubles have not made things any easier in this way." But he never went beyond that in alluding to his private life which he always kept to himself.

He was in touch with nature in the country, but that only aroused his suspicion, and he refused to paint it except from memory: "When I first got here I was damped and dazed by the open air. How do you manage to turn up somewhere, without any preparation, and get down to work at six the next morning?" he enquired of Rouart. And he was constantly

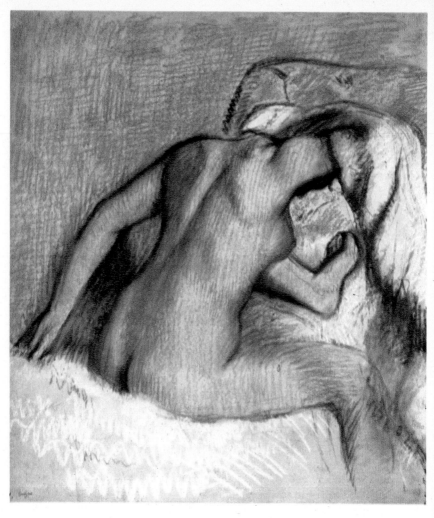

WOMAN DRESSING.
JOSEPH MÜLLER COLLECTION, SOLEURE

complaining of his eyesight: "My eyes no longer focus, or it becomes such a difficult matter that one is tempted to abandon the effort and just go on sleeping."

In 1886 he went back to Naples where he had a house, left him by his uncle, on the slopes of Posilippo. But meeting once

BALLET GIRLS IN THE WINGS (c. 1889)
BÜHRLE COLLECTION, ZURICH

more the family which had played such an important part at the beginning of his career was not as successful as he had expected: "I'm simply a Frenchman who's a nuisance, and the family keep out of my way. Let me get back to my Valkyrie's palace of flames – that's to say my studio and the heat of a decent stove." Again he reverted to that lack of feeling which

69

troubled him more than he would admit: "There's something false in my feelings, in my heart. Those ballet girls have sewn it up in a pink satin bag – a little faded like their dancing shoes." This letter of his to Bartholomé contains a declaration of faith which has often been quoted, as it is the best comment ever made on the austerity of his work: "The same subject needs going over ten times, a hundred times. Nothing in art, not even movement itself, should look like chance."

He kept to his high conception of art even when he had to labour to fulfil a promise, such as that, for instance, which he had made to Faure: "I have to be patient in completing things which waste the time that remains to me – affection and respect for art stop me from scamping them."

Obliged to take the waters at Cauteret, he killed time by writing a number of letters to Ludovic Halévy, Henri Rouart, and Bartholomé. It was from this spa that he went in 1899 with Boldini on an expedition to Spain which seems to have disappointed him and led to a quarrel between them. Yet the Spanish painters gave him even more than he had expected: "Nothing, nothing at all, can give one the least idea of Velazquez." He returned to Paris after a stay in Tangiers where he was reminded of his favourite Delacroix.

He made brief excursions to Belgium, Holland, and England, which do not seem to have made much impression on him. He was constantly setting art against nature. But there is a complexity worthy of Stendhal in a phrase of his after he had heard a flute played in the open air: "Nature is too dull when you come across something really artistic like that. It's when I'm unhappy that the idea of happiness brings tears to my eyes – and at the theatre . . ."

70

WOMEN BATHING (1890)
PRIVATE COLLECTION

But work in his studio was at one and the same time almost his only joy and his constant anguish. Gradually he had dropped his friends, went less into society, less even to the theatre. The Dreyfus case was a burning question to him, as to so many Frenchmen. It finally separated him from his Impressionist friends, who were nearly all for Dreyfus, while he, as he grew older, had become a violent nationalist, including Jews and Protestants in his bitter hostility.

This self-absorption hastened his evolution; he gradually gave up depicting that picturesque side of life which had so long attracted him. He no longer cared to paint laundresses and milliners, nor to go with the girls he knew to a fitting, which used to entertain him at one time.

It is not easy to describe all his experiments, his second thoughts, his reactions, his momentary interest in landscapes, then once again his obsession with his favourite ballet girls or with the race-horses which were no less dear to him.

THE HUMAN ANIMAL

Yet the moment came when this interrupted development attained at last to the series of nude studies in which woman is stripped of all those embellishments which Degas had so long enjoyed painting – the moment when the background no longer mattered or was reduced to a single detail; hip bath, bath, pile of clothes, or chair. Henry Moore has recorded a remark of the painter on a day when he was displaying those nude studies in which the physical creature is stripped and revealed with a complete absence of shame. "There's the human animal doing what matters to her," Degas told him, "a cat licking herself. My women are simple, straightforward creatures who are only concerned with their physical habits: there's one washing her feet – it's as if you were watching through the keyhole."

The female form, bare or clothed in a ballet dancer's skirt, became almost the only thing he studied in the closing years of the century. Most often he used pastel for it, charcoal, or clay and wax. It is impossible to distinguish between the techniques he employed at this period. All that mattered to him was the form which he had to observe in ever greater detail, to emphasize and bring out the essential features.

Those who had become used to his more attractive subjects, his scenes taken from the theatre, the street or shops, even from bawdy houses, were reserved in their welcome to an art which aimed at a bareness of increasing austerity. In fact as the scale of his works increased, the number of figures grew less, and few canvases in his last period show more than one model.

Some have not hesitated to ascribe to Degas' failing eyesight this remarkable determination of his to simplify in his art, whereas it was the result of an evolution whose phases we have tried to point out, and at the cost of unrelenting labours, which took him from *Disasters of Orleans* to these almost abstract forms which, in Huysmans' phrase, evoke "a feeling of precise exoticism."

By then Degas was seventy-five. For twenty-five years he had never left his studio except in the evening for long lonely walks or to go to the few friends from whom he sometimes

73

BALLET GIRLS IN SALMON-PINK SKIRTS (c. 1897)
BÜHRLE COLLECTION, ZURICH

BALLET GIRLS (c. 1895)
PRIVATE COLLECTION, PARIS

accepted invitations into the country. No artist of his generation had been more persevering, nor more strict with himself – always dissatisfied, refusing to give up canvases which he considered unfinished – so much so that Faure, the singer, had to go to law to force him to keep a contract.

He would never have agreed to make public many of the works that were found in cases after his death. But an artist may not always be clear-headed about his own work. It is at least evident that, if his failing eyesight had an effect on his art, this effect was good in that it hastened his evolution by obliging him to abandon everything except the essential. He could never have said, with Cézanne, that "the outline eludes me," for his last works are precisely the most striking both in strength and character, showing that he had at last found himself at the end of a lifetime's experiments devoted wholly to his work. Moreover the sacrifices which he had imposed on himself were only apparent, for real happiness existed for him only inside his studio, nowhere else – which is the reason why he had forbidden the place to everybody except his models, who to him were entirely soulless objects.

Instead of putting them in some conventional posture, he asked them to adopt attitudes to which they were accustomed in their daily life, those which best brought out the play of their muscles; so they twisted their hair, bent down, arched their backs. The painter never let them take any restful pose, but painted them – as he declared in the 1886 exhibition's catalogue – "bathing, washing, drying and wiping themselves, combing their hair or having it combed for them."

In these works he was less concerned with skilful composition than with merciless analysis, as if the painter was trying, if not to degrade woman, at least to reduce her, as he said himself, to her animal nature.

To this great series of nude studies painted towards the close of his life, I owe one of the most memorable experiences of my own:

When Ambroise Vollard, around 1925, set up house in the Rue Martignac, overlooked by the church of St. Cloti!de, he announced that he was opening a gallery on the ground floor of the building in whose annex Georges Rouault was carrying out his remarkable work.

Each time I went there I enquired about the opening date of this gallery, and Vollard, in entire good faith, explained to me the causes of the repeated postponements – the place was not quite ready, the lighting or the colour of the moulding was wrong, the frames he had chosen for the pictures had been delayed.

Years passed and I had given up asking these awkward questions when one evening Vollard, after a dinner to which some friends had been invited to share a West Indian dish, said that he wanted to show them a few pictures. We followed him down to the lower floor where we were greeted with an astounding sight – all the great pastels and emphatic charcoals that Ambroise Vollard had bought from Degas, or that he had obtained in the sales that followed his death, were there. Probably they were the only series of works in his collection that had never been taken out of their cases, where so many masterpieces were stowed away before disappearing, after his death, to America or elsewhere.

For an hour we were able to look at these works that had become a legend, perfectly hung and lighted. I received such an overwhelming impression from them that I could not help saying to the author of *Memoirs of a Picture Dealer* that he had no right to keep so many extraordinary masterpieces to himself. "Yes," he answered, "I'll soon be arranging for the opening of my gallery."

Months and then years went by. Since Vollard's tragic death in 1939, nobody knows what is the fate today of this collection which revealed the culmination of Degas' whole life.

WASHERWOMEN AND HORSE (c. 1902)
LAUSANNE MUSEUM

LAST YEARS

Those years in which he at last achieved his aim were the saddest of his life. His outlook was limited to the walls of his studio – for he always refused to work from nature. So it was the height of paradox when the only showing of his work to which he would agree, at Durand-Ruel's in 1892, was an exhibition of landscapes! But these landscapes were done in his studio, as were those he painted on his return from the famous tour through Burgundy with Bartholomé in a gig, when they covered three hundred and seventy miles in twenty days. Seeing the pictures, Bartholomé was struck by their accuracy: "To think," he exclaimed, "that he never once stopped to look!"

Indeed Degas was only sarcastic at the expense of those landscape painters who worked on the spot: "Draw what has stayed in your memory," he said, "then you'll only bring out what has really struck you, which is all that matters."

In 1893 he went on an extensive tour which took him to Carpentras, to see his friend de Valernes, then on to Switzerland. In 1897 he went to Montauban and asked the mayor of the town for permission to photograph some Ingres sketches in the museum there.

He stayed with the Rouarts at Queue-en-Brie, at his brother's at St. Valéry-sur-Somme, or at Dieppe. Once or twice he took the waters at Mont-Dore. His last serious excursion was to Alsace in September, 1904. After that he seems hardly ever to have left his studio in the Rue Victor Massé, in the heart of Montmartre, which Paul Laffond describes in the following terms:

THREE BALLET GIRLS (1898)
ORDRUPGAARDSAMLINGEN, CHARLOTTENLUND (DENMARK)

"It is impossible to give any idea of the confusion in the place. There were easels overladen with canvases and pastels still being worked over. Other paintings had their faces to the walls, one against another. There were sculptor's stands, tables heaped with piles of clay, wax models that had been begun, then allowed to crumble away; presses for lithographs or etchings, frames for engravings; things that had been used for background detail in one or another of his paintings showed on every side: double basses, violins, hip baths, dresses, ballet dancers' skirts and shoes, a cast of a female form, a conductor's rostrum, a piano, even theatrical properties – a winding staircase used on the stage. All over the place there were tins of colours, pastels, copper plates, chairs with their cane seats broken and old armchairs with torn covers, packets tied up with string, full to bursting. You had to take great precautions not to upset anything if you attempted the journey to the point where Degas worked, which was between a desk, covered with letters and scattered papers, and the stove."

It is true that, in contrast to all this confusion, his own characteristic figure remained clearly defined. But it is no less true that in his old age Degas was no longer quite the excessively critical person he had once been. He was so obsessed with his art that nothing else mattered to him, and he probably never even looked at the masterpieces which he had collected with such enthusiasm over the years. The only picture visible from his bed was one of his own, *Pagans, the Guitar Player* – because, beside the instrumentalist, he had put in a portrait of his father, whose death had been a severe loss to him.

His last years were intensely sad. His misanthropic outlook drove him to turn aside from any movement of affection. All his life he had complained of his eyesight, and it had come to a point when it might be thought that he was only making use of this as a convenient excuse for seeing merely what he wanted to see.

Now it was no longer an excuse, for he was indeed almost blind. Yet he insisted on making his way through Paris, rejecting every offer of company, getting into buses which took him no matter where, or walking about the town in constant danger of being run over each time he crossed the street. When Sacha Guitry wanted him to appear with Renoir, Monet, and Rodin in his film *Our Own People,* he refused, and if in spite of that we can still see the old man going along the pavement, this is because Guitry spent a long time on the look-out, unknown to him, to get his figure into the film.

He received a final blow on the day when he was told that he had to give up his house in the Rue Victor Massé, where he had two floors and had hoped to end his days. The building was to be demolished, and it was in a daze that he saw to the moving of the treasures which he had taken so long to assemble. He even gave up working: "His days were now passed wandering aimlessly about Paris," Vollard recorded. "His steps always brought him back in front of his house which was being pulled down. When the last laths and plaster had been removed and the site boarded up along the pavement, the old man was to be seen looking through cracks in the barrier at the bare ground ... "

His last days prompted his old friend Paul Laffond to some moving lines: "His long hair, quite white, made a halo round him. His beard was white too, his features calm and peaceful ..." In this old man few would have recognised the handsome young man with a somewhat aloof expression shown in the 1857 portrait. Almost blind, he slowly faded away in his house on the Boulevard de Clichy, where the things he had brought from the Rue Victor Massé had not even been unpacked. He was eighty-three.

At seven in the morning of the 26th of September, 1917, he died peacefully. In the middle of the war his death went almost unnoticed. Only a few friends could judge all that was implied in the passing of a man in whom Huysmans saw "a unique and forceful artist, who had no acknowledged predecessor and no real successor." That is open to question, for Degas recognised not only the Renaissance painters as his masters, but Ingres and Delacroix – Chassériau and Puvis de Chavannes too, no doubt.

As for his successors, his influence on Lautrec is undeniable, and such a canvas as *The Supers* (1877) points the way to all the experiments made by that dwarf of genius.

Finally there is no doubt that Bonnard, Vuillard and their friends quite well realised how much originality there was in Degas' method of composition and perspective.

Never properly understood when he was young, Degas stands in the same case forty years after his death. Of course it is only natural that an age which does not like a work of art to have too much finish to it and which reserves its enthusiasm for the art of primitive peoples, should not respond to works in which, as Paul Valéry has said, "toil has wiped out the signs of toil."

Yet it remains surprising that those academic circles which

dictate to contemporary art in no less sectarian a spirit than their predecessors in the Second Empire are unable to realise that Degas was working towards an ever stricter interpretation of pure form and that abstract art which is the only sort that they recognise.

The Tachists have selected Claude Monet as their master. Perhaps some group of young artists will one day free themselves from all prejudice and look at the drawings and pastels which Degas did towards the close of his life – to recognise in him a bold prophet who prepared the way for them.

LIST OF ILLUSTRATIONS

86